SWEET REASON

Also by this author

Pro Patria

Who Killed William Rufus?

Without Consent

To Encourage the Others

Last Call to San Giorgio

Sleeping Dogs

From Portsmouth to Pickwick

The Journey

Made In Cornwall

Angus Harrop and The Bentley Boys

My Country, Right or Wrong

Trial By Jury – Four Plays

Innocent

Advocacy Plus

SWEET REASON

*A glimpse of Lord Birkett,
advocate and speaker*

Nigel Pascoe QC

Copyright © 2018 Nigel Pascoe

All rights reserved, including the right to reproduce this book, or portions thereof in any form. No part of this text may be reproduced, transmitted, downloaded, decompiled, reverse engineered, or stored, in any form or introduced into any information storage and retrieval system, in any form or by any means, whether electronic or mechanical without the express written permission of the author.

The views expressed in this work are solely those of the author and do not necessarily reflect the views of the publisher, and the publisher hereby disclaims any responsibility for them.

ISBN: 978-0-244-74301-7

Front cover image: Ullswater, Lake District, England

PublishNation
www.publishnation.co.uk

Preface

This is a labour of love. Norman Birkett, later Lord Birkett QC was one of the greatest advocates ever to practise at the English Bar. When I was green and in my salad days, I found an LP of him speaking at a Shakespeare birthday lunch in Stratford in 1938 and also, towards the end of his life, at a cricket dinner. As a bar student, I had read his celebrated biography and only regret that I never heard him in the Inner Temple for he died four years before my own call. But that fantastic mellow voice was still there to treasure. There must be a way to keep his name alive for another generation of students and others For arguably he was the best advocate and speaker of his time.

So in the fullness of time, I began I decided to risk a glimpse of Norman Birkett KC in the form of a short performance, no more than an hour. It would not be an impersonation but hopefully there would be occasional inflections for those few who remembered him or who had heard that record. That meant a fairly selective life and case history, but enough to encourage others to dig deeper. It has been put together from widely published sources with a little interpretation. The emphasis is on Birkett the speaker as much as advocate or judge. And I knew from the outset how it had to end. An incredible speech in the House of Lords two days before his death.

This is the point where I had the great good fortune to discuss the idea with an old friend and in every way the perfect source. Peter Birkett QC is the great nephew of the great man and a fellow Bencher of the Inner Temple. We are both former Circuit Leaders. He is a born advocate and gave me some contact indirectly with the family, some of whom came to the

1st performance in December 2016 in the Inn. I am very grateful to him.

This then is the revised script. The performance has always been enhanced by superlative piano playing, not least by David Kingsmill in its first performance. I love performing it and I hope that in time others will do the same. My thanks to all in the Inner Temple who helped me to stage it. No legal thespian could have hoped for more.

The play is dedicated with love to my wife Elizabeth.

Nigel Pascoe QC November 2018

Cue 1 Sailing by - the midnight weather music

Early 1962. Load Birkett, dressed in a dinner jacket, is sitting at a small desk with an old reading lamp, writing in a large notebook.

What is the coefficient of linear expansion of brass?

You know it would be very strange if in the years to come, they remember me for that single opening question. I was prosecuting in a case called Rouse, a most dreadful murder. The defence called a gentleman as a so-called expert and in cross-examination, I simply wanted to test his expertise. Happily for me, he did not know the answer.

I have often been asked what I would have done if he had answered correctly. Probably I would have asked about another non-ferrous metal...provided that I also knew the answer! Never Ask A Question if you don't!

You see, Advocacy has been my life. And watching Lancashire play cricket! The best of Counties with so many wonderful characters. Oh my Hornby and my Barlow long ago. Do you know it? Francis Thompson's most evocative poem - *At Lords*.

The story is that he had been invited there to watch his beloved Lancashire play Middlesex. But he decided instead to stay at home to pen his memories of those Lancastrian batsmen of many years before, meeting the county which had starred WG Grace and his brothers, including GF Grace.

It's Glo'ster coming North, the irresistible,
The Shire of the Graces, long ago!
It's Gloucestershire up North, the irresistible,

And new-risen Lancashire the foe!
[A Shire so young that has scarce impressed its traces,
Ah, how shall it stand before all-resistless Graces ?
O, little red rose, their bats are as maces To beat thee down, this summer long ago!]
This day of seventy-eight they are come up north against thee
This day of seventy eight, long ago!
The champion of the centuries, he cometh up against thee
With his brethren, every one a famous foe.
The long-whiskered Doctor, that laugheth the rules to scorn, while the bowler, pitched against him, bans the day he was born;
And G.F. with his science makes the fairest length forlorn;
They are come from the West to work thee woe!

It is little I repair to the matches of the Southron folk
Though my own red roses there may blow;
It is little I repair to the matches of the Southron folk,
Though the red roses crest the caps, I know.

For the field is full of shadows as I near a shadowy coast,
And a ghostly batsmen plays to the bowling of a ghost,
And I look through my tears on a soundless-clapping host
As the run steelers flicker to and fro, to and fro:
O my Hornby and my Barlow long ago!

I recited that tonight at a cricket dinner in London. The toast was - Cricketers Everywhere. They seemed to enjoy it. Which I must say gave me very great pleasure. And I told them again the story of the cricket supporter who every night prayed for each one of his side's batsmen... 'God bless Edrich, God bless Compton' all the way down the batting order and he was so passionate that he even finished up - 'And God bless leg byes!'

But as you see, I still have to work. To prepare every detail of every speech as if it were my first. One of the great secrets of all advocacy, in or out of court.

Points to his notebook

And I have two speeches now to prepare and very little time to do so. The Inner Temple would like me to talk once more about my life. I was Treasurer there a few years ago. So I suppose I must finish that one first. And tell the truth, of course.

Then I have a very important speech to make in the House of Lords. Manchester Corporation want to take further water from the Lake District. So much at stake for my beloved Ullswater.

Turns notebook back to beginning

So now I need to go back very many years…

Cue 2 Piano
Stand at lectern

Master Treasurer, Members of the Inn. **September 6th 1883.**The day I was born in Ulverston in Furness, in the County of Lancashire. Number 4, Ainsworth Street. And later I went on to grammar school in Barrow in Furness. In case you may have forgotten, that's a sea port on the Cumbrian coast. But as you may appreciate, I think of myself as a Lancastrian through and through.

My father Thomas was a draper with a number of shops and he became a well-established man in the town. My poor mother Agnes died of tuberculosis three years after I was born, as the fourth of five children.

I spent the first twenty four years of my life in that old market town and you know, it is still very dear to me. For it has a charm and a character peculiarly its own.

Now my parents were staunch Non-Conformists - and my father very prominent in the local Methodist Wesleyan congregation. And the Chapel was where I learned to speak.

Cue 3 Hymn - On Jordan's Banks

I became a very regular speaker on the circuit at a young age and for a number of years, I believed that was my calling in life. Over the years, my beliefs have wavered, but my respect remains.

My father married again and my stepmother, also Agnes, continued to make it a happy and united family. And in time I had a new sister, Mary.

I think of my early schooldays at the Ulverston Wesleyan Day school as a most formative influence on my life. Indeed as I look back, it was a time of great happiness and I shall always think with affection of the school and chapel and my home.

Then to the Higher Grade School in Barrow. It was a journey by train - which allowed me to carry out a number of practical jokes on other passengers, about which the less said the better! But I cannot claim great academic success there. One school report put me 7th out of a class of 31, with my two best subjects Spelling and Practical Chemistry. But rather less well in Algebra! So in **1898** aged 15, I left school to start work as an assistant draper in one of my father's shops. My cousin Henry was a fellow apprentice.

By now, I had become quite a popular local preacher. But in a few years, my father came to realize that I was unlikely to be a successful draper. After all, there is not much call for long speeches when you have a shop full of customers! So in **1904**, he allowed me to leave - to become a Minister. Next year, my mentor suggested that I should go to Cambridge to study history and theology. I was now 22.

Well, I applied to Emmanuel College, who offered me a place provided that I passed an entrance examination. Now that meant three very hard months learning Latin and Greek. But, you know, it was a very good discipline for hard work at the Bar! And that is the only way to succeed in our beloved profession. Fortunately I was accepted and Emmanuel first saw me in **October 1907**.

I continued to preach on the local Methodist circuit, and somehow found time for rugby and football and golf. *Golf* - an endlessly distracting pastime! I have played it all my life, But you know, I have to tell you that my handicap today is covered by the Official Secrets Act!

There was, however, another temptation I first spoke at the **Cambridge Union** in my second term. The motion was that "This House would welcome the Disestablishment of the Church of England."

The *Cambridge Review* reported that it was "a most interesting speech." Of course we all know that 'interesting' is a word that covers a multitude of sins!

But after that, I spoke many times at the Union - Home Rule for Ireland - Cruelty to Animals and Secular Education, I recall.

In **1910**, I was elected Secretary and two terms later, President of the Union. On one memorable occasion, I moved a resolution making the former American President, Theodore Roosevelt an Honorary Member, when he visited Cambridge to receive an honorary degree.

"I for my own part, as a member of Emmanuel College, experience this honour in a deepened sense, if that be possible. For Emmanuel is justly proud of its intimate connection with Harvard University and it is for me a matter for personal congratulations to welcome, in the name of this House, one of Harvard's most distinguished sons. It is a good thing for us for us to think, Sir, that for the future the ex-President of the United States will be associated with this House."

The speech was rather well received by Mr Roosevelt and indeed by the union as a whole. You could say, I suppose, that I was on my way.

Cue 4 piano - ragtime

In **1910**, I was fortunate to be awarded First Class Honours in my Theological Special Examination. But it was then that I began to have doubts about my future as a Minister. So I spoke to the University Law Reader about a possible career at the Bar. And on his advice, I took Part Two of the Law Tripos in **1911**.

Then the question for many would-be barristers without the benefit of scholarship or funds. For I could not expect my father to pay for me. I had written to him in some despair thinking of my brother Gilbert and my sisters working hard and earning money -

"I feel like a useless drain on everything. I'm sorry to be such a great burden. It makes me dreadfully unhappy."

So how would I survive? I remember that I tried *The Guardian* and *The Observer* - and eventually I found a job as personal secretary to George Cadbury Junior, who at the time was a well-known philanthropist. My wage was £200 a year, and I planned to hold on to the post until I was called to the Bar.

By then I had joined the Inner Temple and Master Treasurer, I have never made a better decision! But after a month, my salary was raised to £500, and I was offered a permanent position. Very tempting, of course, but I had set my cap elsewhere.

By now, I was active in politics and spoke often on behalf of the Liberal Party. On one occasion, I recall seeking to hold the attention of more than a thousand people for an hour. But I don't suggest that is something you should risk too often! Not, that is, if you want them to stay awake!

In **1912**, I took the first part of the Bar Examination. I seem to recall a temporary setback with the less than fascinating subject of Real Property...but ultimately, I was called to the Bar on **June 4th, 1913**.

Now whilst working as secretary, I had become very close to a girl called Ruth Nilsson, known to everyone as '**Billy**'
There I must confess that my advocacy was not immediately successful...For I had to propose to her several times before she agreed to marry me!

Billy gave up her position at Bourneville to move to London and we were married on the **25ᵗʰ of August 1920**. In time, we had two children, our daughter **Linnea** and our son **Michael**.
It is a very personal matter, of course, but I cannot begin put into words all that that I owe to Billy, my children and grandchildren.

After my call to the Bar, I moved in **1914** to Birmingham. You see, because of my stint with George Cadbury, I now had some connections there and I was able to join the chambers of John Hurst, who was a leading junior on the Midland Circuit, which of course I also joined.

However that year, I also contracted tuberculosis and I was declared unfit for military service. And I had to return to Ulverston for six months to recover. So undoubtedly my career was aided by the outbreak of World War I.

Cue 5 *Roses of Picardy – begin softly*

For many of the younger and fitter barristers were called up for war service. *pause* And some did not return.

'In Flanders fields the poppies blow
Between the crosses, row on row,
That mark our place; and in the sky
The larks, still bravely singing, fly
Scarce heard amid the guns below.
We are the Dead. Short days ago
We lived, felt dawn, saw sunset glow,
Loved and were loved, and now we lie
In Flanders fields.
Take up our quarrel with the foe:
To you from failing hands we throw

The torch; be yours to hold it high.
If ye break faith with us who die
We shall not sleep, though poppies grow
In Flanders fields.'
I do not forget. No one should. *pause*

Now during my time in Birmingham, I still continued my work as a Minister, and I was preaching regularly at the Baptist People's Chapel.
And it was at this time that I started to get good Defence work. Indeed in **1919**, I was advised by a local Circuit Judge to move to London to advance my career.

Initially I must confess that I was very hesitant. Competition in London was on quite a different scale, and if I failed there, I would have lost everything that I had built up in Birmingham. But a case that I undertook in **1920** made the decision for me.

Cue 6 Music

I acted as a junior for the prosecution in the so-called Green Bicycle Murder case against Edward Marshall-Hall and tried in Leicester. Indeed I was led both by the Attorney General of the day, Sir Gordon Hewart and an old circuit friend, Henry Maddocks, by then a silk.

I will not trouble you with the details, but sufficient to say, the Prosecution was unsuccessful. But somehow I managed to impress Marshall-Hall and he offered me a place in his chambers in London.
I had no London solicitors of my own. But the clerk helped enormously by using me as a junior to Marshall-Hall whenever possible. It made a huge difference.

Now you may be interested if I say a few words about Edward Marshall-Hall - a towering advocate I n all senses and a most distinguished member of this Inn.

You know that it was said of him that he threw the cloak of his own personality around his clients and he utterly captivated juries.

I shall always remember the moment when he came into court at Leicester Castle. He brought with him a strange magnetic quality, his name a household word and a faint murmur ran from floor to gallery. He came with all the prestige of the greatest criminal defender of the day and every eye was fixed upon him. He was a very handsome man, with a noble head and expressive face. F E Smith's comment cannot be bettered -

"Nobody could be as wonderful as Marshall Hall then looked." To that was added perhaps the greatest gift of all in the armoury of an advocate – a most beautiful speaking voice.
Later in life, I tried to pin down his success in a picture of Six Great Advocates, which was also broadcast.

I need to say a little about my **political career**, which flourished and waned at the will of the electorate. Rather a mixed picture. My father had been a supporter of the Liberal Party, and I had helped him campaign during the **1906 General Election**.

Then in **1911**, I was invited to become the Liberal candidate for Cambridge, but then I could not possibly afford to do so.
But in the **1923 General Election**, I was finally elected for Nottingham East, overcoming a Conservative majority of 4,000.

I do remember my **maiden speech**. I responded to a proposal by a Labour Party member in favour of a State Pension for widows with children - and wives, whose husbands were unable to work because of injury. I called it humane and beneficial.

"I support this with all my heart because not merely will it remove the haunting sense of insecurity with which so many widows are faced today, but it is a very definite and practical charter for the children. If there was one note that received wide commendation, so far as I am able to judge, in my election, it was that which laid stress on better opportunities for the rising generation.

There were many men who were prepared to stand up and say 'I never had much of a chance myself. I was always handicapped from the beginning; but if anything can be done to give a better chance to the children who are now coming on, I shall be satisfied.'

Then I went rather further. I suggested that Pensions should be considered also for unmarried mothers, deserted and in some cases, divorced wives.

That may have been rather presumptuous. As it was said of another first effort, not so much of a maiden but *[mimic Winston]* a *brazen hussey* of a speech! Certainly it attracted a lot of interest at the time.

But the Bar came first. So my appearances in the House of Commons were rare - although I do remember once spending all night in a Parliamentary session that ended at 6 in the morning and then going straight off to court. Which is not something that I would recommend on a regular basis!

In **1924**, I applied to become **King's Counsel**.
In those days, barristers who were also Members of Parliament had a greater chance of success. So it proved. On April 15th of that year, I was sworn in as one of His Majesty's Counsel, learned in the law.

Naturally it was a very proud moment for a Lancashire boy and I cherish the kind letters that I received.

You know, The Law can be a very warm and friendly place and I felt on top of the world.

And as I look back, those early years in silk were some of the happiest days of my life. I wonder sometimes why I ever moved away.

And my financial position certainly improved. Nothing like the fees today, but let me give you figures. In my first year as a King's Counsel, I earned £8,000 and that was double my fees as a junior the previous year.

So the gamble of taking silk had paid off. But if you know in your heart that you must press forward in life, don't let anyone put you off.

In **1924**, an extraordinary case called **Campbell** brought down the Labour minority government. It was believed that backbench pressure had caused the Government of Ramsay Macdonald to suspend the prosecution of a British Communist newspaper for Incitement to mutiny.

And I went back to **Nottingham East** to campaign for re-election But this time I faced a far more difficult task than in 1923.

The Conservative candidate was much stronger and the left-wing vote was split, because a noted Communist was standing.

Then, a few days before the election, an extraordinary letter was published - apparently addressed to the Communist Party. It spoke of 'Organising Uprisings in British Colonies.' It caused an uproar and it drove many voters to the right.

That is why so many Liberal members of Parliament in October 1924 lost their seats to Conservatives. Including me.

Back then full time at the Bar, before I again risked the hazards of a parliamentary career

Whilst working with Marshall Hall, I was involved in several notable criminal cases. But it was a matrimonial issue which bought me a welcome burst of publicity.

It was known as **the Bachelor's Case** and you may be interested in the unusual way it developed.

Essentially it was a High Court financial dispute in 1925 between Lieutenant Colonel Ian Dennistoun and his former wife Dorothy.

When they had divorced, the Colonel could not pay her ancillary relief. So instead he promised he would provide for his former wife in the future *when he had the money.*

Sometime after they had divorced, he married a wealthy lady Almina, Countess of Caernarvon, the widow of Lord Caernarvon.

Under her husband's will, she was now very well provided for and in turn then provided for her new husband.

So it might be said that now the Colonel *did* have the money to pay. You can see where the case was leading.

After hearing about this change in his fortunes, his former wife Dorothy demanded the alimony that she had been promised.

But the new wife Lady Caernarvon took a very different view. Indeed she saw this understandable claim as a form of blackmail. And it was Lady Caernarvon who persuaded her new husband to take his former wife to court. It was a jury action.

<u>Mr Justice McCardie</u>, who tried the case, called it
"the most bitterly conducted litigation I have ever known."

Marshall Hall and I represented Lady Caernarvon and the Colonel. A leading divorce barrister represented the former wife. Mrs Dennistoun.

You may think that, on the merits, we would have an uphill task and begin with, the case was going badly for us. For once, Marshall Hall did not succeed in cross examination and an illness had made him irritable and short-tempered. On the advice of the clerk, he asked me to make the closing speech.

Now I am sure you will understand the challenge and the opportunity for me that that provided. I knew that I had to make the Jury feel sorry for Lady Carnarvan and reject outright the claim of the former wife. I finished on a very rhetorical note.

"Members of the Jury, is it to be suggested that Lady Carnarvan should say - 'I will give you my money and you shall give it to the woman who divorced you?'

That would be repugnant to morals, to common sense and everything else. Blackmail takes many forms but this is about the most dreadful form that it can take.

There are issues in this case of exceeding gravity. People in the position of Lady Carnarvan do not face the ordeal of publicity during nearly three weeks - for nothing."

So it was that an initially hostile jury decided to disregard the agreement of the Colonel to pay ancillary relief to his former wife.

In those days, such matters were widely reported and I made the front page of the Daily Mail evening edition. I received some very welcome publicity and some kind words.

The consequence of the case and its coverage was that I came to the attention of a number of London solicitors and my earnings rose substantially.

But I had not yet wearied of politics. At the general election in **May 1929**, I was returned as MP for Nottingham East with a majority of nearly 3,000.

Ramsay MacDonald, who was Prime Minister of the minority Government, offered me the position of <u>Solicitor General</u> if I would defect to the Labour Party, as they had few experienced lawyers in the House of Commons.

My colleague, **William Jowett**, did defect, in exchange for the position of Attorney General.

I took a rather high-minded view. I said that I could not change my politics in twenty five minutes and even if the Liberal party should disintegrate completely, I would not be seen taking refuge in the Labour arc. Not tactful perhaps, but that is how I felt at the time.

But from then on, my attendance was much more frequent in the House of Commons. **Sir John Simon** and I became leading Liberal party legal spokesman.

I remember launching a stirring attack on one clause of the Finance Act 1930 - which brought an unexpected response from a very famous voice [*Churchill – mimic voice*]

"I have rarely heard a speech more precisely directed at the object under debate, more harmoniously attuned to the character of committee discussion, than the excellent statement the Honourable and learned Gentleman has just made."

Winston, no less. Always a generous opponent.

Later, I was offered again the post of Solicitor General and again I refused and this time, **Stafford Cripps** was appointed.

When the Liberal party returned to power in 1931, it was in coalition with the Conservatives and National Labour as part of Ramsay MacDonald's National Government.

It is fair to say that it was thought that I would be offered the same post again.

But by the time it came to be discussed, the Liberals had exceeded their ministerial quota, which they had agreed to, as part of the coalition.

I was offered a non-legal office, but I said that I couldn't contemplate a post that meant me giving up my practice.

So to my last Commons chapter. In 1931, after an economic crisis, the King dissolved Parliament and I returned to Nottingham to defend my seat.

I had the same Conservative opponent, but this time the Conservative party's support of protectionism met with strong approval from the electorate.

You see, many electors were employed in Industries which had suffered after the institution of our policy of Free Trade.

So my opponent was successful in October, with a majority of over 5,000 votes.

Disillusioned with the circumstances, I bade farewell to East Nottingham and retired from front line politics.

They say that all political careers ultimately end in disappointment and I'm very much inclined to agree.

And so yet again, I returned full-time to my beloved Bar.

Cue 7 Music SIT

Time, I think for Criminal matters and the question that I told you about earlier.

In 1930, I prosecuted in the Rouse case, the so-called blazing car murder case. Two young men were returning home in Northampton, when they saw a bright light in the distance and a man coming out of a ditch on the side of the road. He looked back at the lights and said

"Looks like somebody's had a bonfire."

They ran towards the light and saw it was a burning car and they promptly fetched a policeman.

When the fire died down, a body was found inside the boot. The face was so charred that it was impossible to determine its identity. But the number plate on the car was still intact and it was traced to a Mr Alfred Rouse.

He was arrested and appeared eventually at Northampton Crown Court in January 1931, charged with the murder of an unknown man.

Appearing for the defence was Donald Finnimore, later a most excellent High Court Judge. I represented the Crown, together with Richard Elwes.

The defence had serious difficulties.

When the defendant was arrested, he had said words to the effect that he was very glad it was over" and also - "I'm responsible."

He also said that the car engine had been off at the time of the fire. Of course, that ruled out the possibility of accidental ignition.

However, when he gave evidence, a rather different version emerged. He claimed that he had given an unknown man a lift and then found that he was running out of petrol.

So he asked the passenger to take the spare can in the car and fill up the fuel tank, whilst he went to the side of the road to relieve himself.

Whilst there, he said that he heard a large explosion - and saw a huge flame and became convinced that the petrol tank would explode. That caused him to run away as fast as possible - which was the point where he ran into the two young men on the road.

The defence Expert Witness was called to add credibility to the possibility that there *had* been an accidental explosion, which is why my questions about linear expansion proved fertile territory to undermine his credibility.

The jury took only fifteen minutes to convict him of murder.

There is a tailpiece to the case..

After his appeal had been rejected by both the Court of Appeal and the Home Secretary of the day, he admitted the killing..

One theory was that he had done so in an attempt to fake his own death. But despite his admission of guilt, the identity of the victim was never discovered.

Then in 1934, I acted as counsel in the second of the two **Brighton train murders.**

On reflection, I think it was my greatest triumph in a capital case. But when you have heard the whole story, you may take a different view.

The facts were very gruesome. In June, a woman's torso had been found in a suitcase in Brighton railway station. Later her legs were discovered at King's Cross, but her head and arms were never found.

Now by then, another woman by the name of **Violet Kaye** had also disappeared, so the appearance of the first woman's body caused greater scrutiny on her disappearance.

On July 14th, the Police interviewed Violet Kaye's boyfriend, **Tony Mancini**. He convinced them that the dead woman could not possibly be Violet.

The part corpse had by now been identified as around 35 years old and five months pregnant, whilst Violet Kaye was 10 years older.

Violet Kaye herself had last been seen alive on May 10, looking distressed in the doorway to the house and she had been due to visit her sister in London.

On May 11th her sister received a telegram. It read

"GOING ABROAD. GOOD JOB. SAIL SUNDAY. WILL WRITE. VI."

All in capital letters.

The post office clerks could not remember who had sent it. However Experts testify that the handwriting on the telegram had similarities to the writing on a menu written by Tony Mancini.

On May 14th, with the help of another man, Mancini moved his belongings from the house which he had shared with Violet Kaye. They included a large trunk, which was too heavy to move by hand.

Mancini told people that he had broken up with her and that she had moved to Paris and that before she left, he had beaten her.

Later he had said to a friend -

"What is the good of knocking a woman about with your fists? You only hurt yourself. You should hit her with a hammer same as I did, then chop around."

To make matters even worse for the Defence, a hammer head was later found in the rubbish at his old house.

I have said enough perhaps to indicate that there were likely to be formidable problems defending Mancini. But worse was to come.

After the police had left on July 14, Mancini took the train to London. When the police arrived back next morning, they couldn't find him, but they *did* find Violet Kaye's body decomposing in that heavy trunk.

Immediately they sent out a countrywide call for him to be arrested and he was picked up near London. When he was interviewed, he said that he was not guilty and that he had returned home to find Kaye dead.

Then, fearing that with his criminal record he would not be believed, he had hidden the body in the trunk.

When he was in prison, his solicitor had phoned me and asked me to represent him. No easy task!

It is true that there were some limited flaws in the prosecution case. And I emphasised the affectionate nature of the relationship between Violet Kaye and Mancini at times before her death.

On the other hand, there was strong forensic evidence that he had in fact committed the crime. That included marks of blood on Mancini's clothing.

But after the jury had been out for 2 ½ hours, he was found Not Guilty.

At the time, it seemed a great defence forensic triumph.

But – and here is the point for you - before he died, Mancini confessed to the murder.

And how did I feel about that? How would you feel?

There can be only one answer. No advocate should ever blame himself for doing his job. We are not judges. We start with the presumption of innocence and then just deal with the evidence as best we may.

This jury were not satisfied that the case had been proved beyond all reasonable doubt. And that is the end of the matter.

In **May 1937**, I was appointed Chairman of a committee concerning **Abortion**, which was set up by the Minister of Health and the Home Secretary. And that occupied me for two years.

In the Summer of that year, 1937, I was asked to represent the English Bar in Canada, speaking in Ottawa about our Administration of Justice

Then on **April 23rd 1938**, as the storm clouds drifted over Europe, I spoke in Stratford on Avon at a civic lunch.

STAND at lectern

I proposed the toast to the Immortal Memory of William Shakespeare and I was conscious of the forebodings of the time.

I said that he was thought of as not only belonging to the world but also as a great Englishman and a most devoted lover of his native land

'And today we think of him in that capacity when we remember *"This precious stone set in the silver sea"*

And that immortal phrase, when men were bound together in the face of danger,
"We few, we happy few, we band of brothers"

And Mr Mayor, it is an inspiring thing to think of him here in Stratford, possibly speaking the Warwickshire dialect;

all his life loving this countryside where he was born, with a passionate and enduring love;
delighting in its sense and sounds;
finding great pleasure in the flowers of the fields - and letting his imagination play upon their quaint names.

Making the great adventure into London,
Working hard and making many friends; spending many jovial, even convivial evenings with them.
Winning the esteem of his colleagues and his contemporaries.

And then - after 20 years of consummate labour in London - dearest touch of all - retiring to that place where his affections were,
to end his days in touch with those scenes and sights and sounds and sense from whence his imagination had first dated.

And if it be true, Mr Mayor, that The Tempest was the last of the plays and that some of it, at least, was written in Stratford, it is a most fascinating thing to speculate on the fact that,
not very far from where we are met here today,
Shakespeare, perhaps, took his solemn farewell of that great field of imaginative activity in which he has spent so many years

and in the sublimest passage, as I think, in all plays, indeed as I think, in all literature, he said ...

'You do look my friend in a moved sort
As if thou art dismayed.
Be cheerful, sir.
Our revels now have ended.
These our spirits, as I foretold you,
Have melted into air, into thin air

And like the ghostly fabric of our dreams
The cloud capped temples
The great globe itself
Yea all that we inherit shall dissolve
And like the ghostly fabric of our dreams,
leave not a wrack behind.
We are such stuff as dreams are made of
And our little life is rounded with a sleep.'

In Ben Johnson's words,
'he was not of an age but for all time'

Cue 8 Music SIT

After the outbreak of **World War 11** in 1939, I became a member of a committee advising the Home Secretary on the detention of suspected enemy agents. We dealt with more than 1,500 cases in two years. The work was unpaid, but in June 1941, I received a Knighthood.

I also delivered weekly Radio broadcasts using the title 'Onlooker' after the Friday night news, This was to counter the broadcasts of William Joyce, who was known as Lord Haw Haw.

The first broadcast took place in February 1940, and I like to believe they were something of a morale boost during the so-called **Phony War.**

[to audience] I must tell them how I left the Bar

I had been offered appointment to the **High Court** first in **1928**, but I had turned it down. I wasn't really drawn to judicial office...I loved the Bar too much.

But after the death of a High Court judge in October **1941**, the Lord Chancellor offered me that opportunity.

At the time, I thought that it was my public duty to join the bench and so I was sworn in on the **11th of November 1941**.
I was deeply touched that my old and celebrated senior clerk **Edgar Bowker** chose to come with me, at considerable financial sacrifice to himself.

My great friend **Pat Hastings** wrote -

My dear Norman.
I have just heard your news which makes me very sad. Never again to have the joyful battles for which I have been hoping for many a long day.
However for the sake of the bench, I am very glad. I know you will make a judge of whom we shall all be proud and above all, one to whom we shall all be devoted – - and amongst all who appear before you, there will be none who will wish you greater happiness than your devoted friend,
Pat Hastings.

What did I tell you about friendship at the Bar?

So, you may ask, an ambition fulfilled? A sense of achievement? Many would think so. But I said that I would tell you the truth.

I did not enjoy my time as a High Court Judge. Frankly I missed the limelight of being an advocate.

Speaking means so much to me and it was Francis Bacon who observed that an over-speaking Judge is no well-tuned cymbal.

Mind you, some, I believe, say that I was quite a popular judge, although I felt - that I was too weak in my judgment.

The truth is that I did not want to hurt people's feelings. Hardly a recommendation for judicial office!

After my appointment, I became unwell. And in **1942**, I suffered from depression.

Cue 9 Dark Music

Now I am able to speak frankly about such matters, At the Bar you are so caught up with the details and intricacies of a case that you have very little time for introspection.

And remember, barristers rarely admit to being ill, foolish though that may be.

But when that pressure is lifted and you find yourself with a new challenge at odds with all you care about most - in my case, to speak and to command, why that can be very hard to bear.

It is a terrible thing not to be able to do that which you know that you can do so well.

It is like being laid upon one's side whilst the stream of life goes past you.

But in time those feelings passed for a while - and I pressed on.

For several weeks in **1943**, I sat in the **Court of Appeal** before going on Assize. Then after a few weeks, I became physically ill - a combination of heart disease and pneumonia, and I returned home to recover.

I suffered from more illness over the next year. I considered resigning as a judge, as by then I felt that I could no longer trust my abilities to sit.

Not that all my cases lacked interest or significance. For example, they included **Constantine v Imperial Hotels Ltd.** That is, Learie Constantine, the great West Indian Cricketer.
That reaffirmed the common law principle that innkeepers must not refuse accommodation to guests without just cause. In passing, it was a rejection of racism and a good man was vindicated.

But then – then came a turning point in my life, which marked me and eventually ate into my very being.

Cue 10

On **30 August 1945**, I received a letter from the Lord Chancellor asking me to serve as the British judge at the **Nuremberg** Trials of German War Criminals.

I accepted, saying it was "a great honour to be selected".

However when I went to London to discuss it, I was informed that the Foreign Office wanted a more senior judge to be in attendance, ideally a Law Lord.

But since no Law Lord was available, they had requested that a Judge from the Court of Appeal should be appointed.

Lord Justice Lawrence was finally selected as the main British judge, and I was offered the position of Alternate Judge for the trials. I would have no vote in proceedings.

I accepted, although I must admit with rather less enthusiasm than I had shown when accepting the original offer.

The trials ran from **October 1945** to **September 1946**, and although I did not have a vote, I know that my opinion was given weight.

I had kept a detailed diary during the tribunal and noted the very different performances of advocates and the particular success of our own.

After we returned home, thanks came from the Lord Chancellor. He spoke of "vindicating our conceptions of an impartial trial under the rule of law." Wise words. And yes, I did feel a sense of satisfaction and even pride to have been a part of such an historic process Who would not?

Lord Justice Lawrence was made a Baron for his work at Nuremberg.

But at that time, I...[*Birkett struggles with his feelings*] I received nothing.

Now I know that we can all be over-sensitive about such matters and no one more than me. But that slight, as it seemed to me at the time, pushed me again into depression. The black dog, as Churchill called it.

However eventually, I was made a **Privy Counsellor** in the **1947** Birthday Honours list.

But judicial promotion continued to elude me. And sadly, I continued to be unhappy with my work as a Judge.

I wrote in my Diary – "I cannot recapture the joy of achievement I used to experience at the Bar. I am nervous of myself, without much confidence in my judgment and hesitant about my sentences and damages and things of that kind. I have felt no glow of achievement in any summing up, though none of them have been bad." And so in **1948**, again I was struck by depression.

You know, I need to be completely honest. That year, Sir Alfred Thompson Denning and Sir John Singleton were both appointed to the Court of Appeal ahead of me. And again - it *hurt*.

So in **July 1949**, I went to the Lord Chancellor and we discussed the possibility of my own appointment to the Court of Appeal. Discussed, yes - but the matter was not resolved.

In **May 1950**, the Lord Chancellor offered me a peerage. without salary. But I refused. The truth is that I lacked the means to survive without paid employment.

Then in **August 1950**, while speaking at a conference in Washington D.C., I received a telegram from the Lord Chancellor offering me an appointment to the **Court of Appeal** and immediately I wired back my acceptance.

In **October** of that year, I was sworn in and I heard my first case the following day. Perhaps this new challenge would lift my spirits…

The truth was very different. I found the work in the Court of Appeal dull, and my disappointment increased the longer I worked.

As in the High Court, I felt uncertain about my judgements and unsure as to whether I was having an impact on the law at all.[
But the Judiciary, as a whole, were understanding and talked of a mix of humanity and common sense, which some said was beneficial to the Court.

So I stayed on until **1956**, when my long service as a judge allowed me to draw a pension. Later I sat as a **Law Lord** until **1961**.

But I would not like to leave you with the impression that all my work lacked interest.

For example, in **1957** I became Chairman of a Committee of Privy Counsellors holding an inquiry into the Home Secretary's use of **telephone tapping**. I drafted a report supporting their use.

Then in December of that year, a letter arrived from the Prime Minister offering me a **peerage**. I accepted, and my name appeared in the New Year Honours list and I was created **Baron Birkett, of Ulverston in the County of Lancaster.**

A great moment for a Lancashire boy.

So I took my seat in the **House of Lord**s on the **20th of February 1958**. A chance to do that which I most enjoyed; to speak again and outside the narrow framework of the Judiciary. And time to speak more about those subjects which have been so dear to me all my life.

Charles Dickens, for example, and cricket and the English countryside. And I would stress the value in life of Companionship.

You know, it was Lawrence Sterne who once said that it is very nice to have a companion on the road if only to point out how the shadows lengthen as the sun goes down.

And it was George Elliot who so beautifully captured the same theme -
'It is hard to believe… that anything is "worthwhile" unless there is some eye to kindle in common with our own, some brief word uttered now - and then to imply that what that is infinitely precious to us is precious alike to another mind.'

In **1958**, I was also awarded an honorary degree by my old University. The speaker was rather more graceful than the anonymous Judge who had once called my advocacy a positive menace to Justice!

In **February 1959**, I appeared on the first episode of the BBC television program *Face to Face*.

John Freeman was a very skilled questioner and he pressed me about my feelings as a Judge. Why had I first turned it down?

'Because I wasn't really drawn to the judicial office. I loved the Bar so much. It wasn't the money, but I loved the life of the Bar, and I think - you know the life of a judge, and I've proved it since, is a bit remote and a bit lonely.

To be quite honest, sometimes when I listened to cases being conducted, I felt how much I would like to be down there doing it.' I had never spoken a truer word.

I tried to sit as regularly in the House of Lords as possible, and I made my maiden speech in **April 1959** on the subject of crime in the United Kingdom.

In **1961**, I was again invited by the BBC to give a series of talks on the BBC Home Service on **"Six Great Advocates"**.
I picked Edward Marshall-Hall, my old friend Pat Hastings, Edward Clarke, Rufus Isaacs, Charles Russell and the incomparable Thomas Erskine.

Birkett closes book

And that will bring my audience in the Inn up to date.

Which simply leaves my speech in the House of Lords about Ullswater.

Forgive me if I try to do a few minutes more tonight. I must change their minds...I am sure you will understand.

Cue 11 Music
Birkett bends his head over his desk

STAND at lectern

My Lords, I have been waiting, I must say a little eagerly, for the moment when I could rise and say that I oppose the Second Reading of this Bill, and to make it quite plain that the opposition is confined to Part III, the waterworks clause. I hope that it will be seemly on my part to say to the noble Lord, Lord

Jessel, that he is to be congratulated upon the fairness and moderation with which he stated his case in introducing the Bill.

I hope to make, in the course of my observations this afternoon, a convincing reply to the various points which have been raised.

In the Guardian newspaper—which is of special interest in Manchester—the leading article headed "Storm over Ullswater" concluded:
"The final decision ought probably to be taken on **larger** issues - Ullswater is in a National Park, and is indeed one of the most beautiful parts of that park. It must remain unspoiled."

That is my theme this afternoon, and I hope to make it convincing to the House.

Your Lordships will have seen in The Times the letter signed by four distinguished Members of this House, which concluded "But we wonder whether they have made any really serious attempt to search for alternative sources outside the National Park for the water which they reckon they need. And we hope that a decision may be taken even now that they should undertake this as a next step undertake this as a next step....
and that, until this water problem can be looked at as a whole, their present proposals, for which there would appear to be no imperative urgency, should not be proceeded with."

The last quotation I should like to make is from the very valuable letter, I thought, of the noble Earl, Lord Woolton, in The Times of this morning.

"Water is one of the essentials of our lives and the more we improve our standard of living—and particularly our sanitation—the greater will be the demand we make on water supply and the keener will be the competition for the easy sources of supply."

Are these issues to be left to the chance of who gets in first?

If it is true that the Government proposes to introduce legislation dealing with this subject, ought not Parliament tell the public water authorities to wait until we get a comprehensive scheme, and is not this particularly the case where a National Park is involved, and where all the public authorities of the neighbourhood concerned are objectors?"

With regard to the speech of the noble Lord, Lord Jessel, your Lordships will notice that from time to time he put in words to the effect that Manchester **cannot wait**; that this must be done **without delay**;
But is there anything to prevent the Manchester Corporation at a future date from coming back, after a suitable opportunity for consultation and reflection?

With very great respect, I would say that this is not an urgent matter, and I say it deliberately and advisedly.

The supplies of water from the first scheme Manchester undertook in the Peak District, with Thirlmere and with Haweswater—from all those sources—are 126 million gallons a day, available to the Manchester Corporation.

It was stated at the Town's meeting in Manchester that 104 million gallons per day are used by Manchester and the waterworks allied with Manchester. The rate of increase, which is purely an estimate, is 3 million gallons per day per year.

And on that footing, every additional drop of water which is sought by this Bill by the Manchester Corporation is not to be used at least until 1970. On their own case, they do not need any additional water until 1970.

What is the use of coming to this House and pleading this as a matter "of urgency; there can be no delay; it is vital if we are to fulfil these obligations which Parliament has laid upon us"?

Of course Parliament laid upon them obligations.

It was one of the terms by which they got their immense power. Parliament said, in effect, "We shall not let you take the water from Thirlmere unless you undertake to supply, as you can quite conveniently, people en route".

And **now** they put it as a kind of <u>virtue -</u>
"It is urgent to look at what we have to do by way of responsibility", when it was a <u>condition</u> by which they **had** to do it.

And they say, with pious hope, "We so earnestly desire to fulfil these needs". Of course they do; they <u>must.</u>

And then they say, at the last, "In all these circumstances the Lake District is our only hope".

I have heard some specious pleading in my time, and made it, I freely acknowledge; but that has also given me the experience to recognise it when I see it.

I suggest that the note of urgency imported into the the speech of the noble Lord, Lord Jessel, is merely pleading. They do not need the water until 1970.

If they get the 40 million or 50 million gallons under this Bill, and it begins to be expended in 1970, by 1985 or thereabouts they will want *more* water.

Where are they going for that? Ullswater?

The Chairman of the Waterworks has given an undertaking, I understand, that they will seek no more from Ullswater.

It is like the extempore speech of which Lord Hewart used to speak; it is not worth the paper it is written on.

The Manchester Corporation can no more bind its successors than anybody else can.

Manchester is saying now:
"Give us the powers, let us do this, and the amenities of Lakeland and of Ullswater will be quite untouched and quite undiminished"

There was a phrase used by the noble Viscount, the Leader of the House, the other day in a debate. The phrase is a biblical phrase and very effective:
"By their fruits ye shall know them".

We have only to look at Thirlmere as it is to-day We have only to look at Haweswater as it is to-day. Both lovely lakes have been murdered.

They are now dead water reservoirs: no human life; sterile shores; why! even the afforestation of the Manchester Corporation prevents proper access to the fell-side until intervention is made in that behalf.

And they come to this House with this Bill now and say, "We are only going to destroy a valley, if you can call it destruction;
In Bannisdale, we are going to build a huge reservoir with a mighty dam; but it is a secluded valley, very few people go there "—as though seclusion and solitude was not one of the things people wanted!

They say, "We are only going to take up our weir from Ullswater; we are not going to damage the amenities; you need have no fear."

Whereas we know in truth and in fact that if you raise the level of the lake and hold it there fifteen days, there may be a <u>flood</u>.

Under this Bill it can be taken for a certainty— everybody with any experience of Lakeland knows it—that these lovely shores of Ullswater, where people picnic, where the ponies come down, will be just sterile shores like one sees at Thirlmere.

May I suggest what is the question your Lordships will be asked to determine?

It is a simple one. It is

<u>At this moment, February, 1962, shall the Manchester Corporation be permitted to invade Lakeland for the third time, to impound its waters, to pour them into its aqueducts, - or not?</u>

That is the question of principle about which Your Lordships are asked to make up your minds.

And the great overriding principle which never operated before in the case of Thirlmere or in the case of Haweswater arises now—namely, are we going to allow this in a National Park?

The National Parks were set up so that the scenic beauty should be preserved and that the enjoyment of the parks should be for all people in all times.

That is the principle which is before your Lordships here this afternoon. To say "There have been many invasions there. Here is one more", is a *pitiful* argument.

Before I sit down I shall make one plea that Your Lordships will assert that Parliament has said that these areas, few though they be, in our land shall be preserved inviolate;
that they shall not be invaded by this or the other undertaking; that that principle shall be maintained in its fullness by the Members of this House.

I know perfectly well what people feel about it.

We are unaccustomed to use words such as "This precious stone set in the silver sea ". We think it, but we rarely say it.

I am greatly tempted when it comes to defending the beauty of the English Lakelands—so small, so lovely, so vulnerable upon that account—to call to aid the great Wordsworth, the great men who have lived there and who have had the power to set down upon the printed pad what scenic beauty can mean to the individual life and to the life of the nation.

So far from saying in this House "It has been done many times. Let it be done once more", surely the argument should be, "It has been too many times already; do not let us add to it".

There are two things I do want to say before I sit down.
I want to make it quite clear that the opposition here are not saying that Manchester shall not have the water. The opposition here say that Manchester must have the water.

May I be pardoned for one more quotation to sustain that particular argument?—it is again from the Guardian:
"Until there is a national water policy, no individual authority or group of authorities should be allowed to pre-empt Ullswater."

But a proper survey of resources in the north of England, as elsewhere, must be made first.

Future demand must also be examined. Only then can it be judged who should draw on Ullswater.

What is needed is something on a much larger scale.

We have had the White Paper, and it would appear that a Government scheme is certainly in contemplation.

I think a central authority is envisaged, and certainly it is suggested that all the water supplies of this country should be surveyed and a national policy created.

There is a further one which I think is even more important.

What steps are to be taken in regard to the distillation of seawater which may be something which is just around the corner?

All these things may be a little in the future, and that is why I emphasised as strongly as I could the fact that there is no note of urgency about this matter at all.

My Lords, I suppose that to-day we have a House which is as full as any I have had the privilege of addressing, and I suppose this would be the moment for what I would call my peroration.

I leave it on one side; I do not feel equal to a peroration on a theme like this at this moment, and will content myself by saying this.

Your Lordships will have a great opportunity this evening when the Division is taken to vindicate the right of the House to say on any measure such as this,

"Thus far and no farther. Go away. Come again another day, if you will. But in the meantime, do that which ought to have been done before.

Produce the hydrological data on which the House can come to a proper decision. Until that is done, you have no right whatever to invade the sanctity of a National Park".

That principle will be invaluable if it is established by the House.

And it involves this other principle, too.

It will urge upon the Government the immediate necessity of producing that national scheme which, in the words of the noble Lord Morrison of Lambeth, will give natural justice to every interest."

My Lords, I beg to oppose the Second Reading.

MOVE TO SECOND LECTERN

NP It was his last speech and perhaps his greatest. When the votes were announced, Lord Birkett and his supporters had won by 70 votes to 36. And cheers greeted the result of the Division.

The next morning, he read with delight the newspaper reports, letters and telegrams of congratulation which had begun to arrive.

But shortly after lunch, he collapsed and was taken to hospital.

The doctors discovered that he had ruptured an important blood vessel and immediate surgery was needed, although it could not have cured him.

Mercifully, he died early in the morning on **February 10th 1962**, allowed, in the words of Lady Birkett, to slip away with the minimum of pain and the minimum of worry.

Again in her words, "It was the way for him to go on the very crest of the wave."

Cue 12 Music - Nimrod

NP What then should be the epitaph for this supremely talented man? Surely it is very simple.

The Times wrote of a warm and kind-hearted man and possessed of great public spirit.

A lawyer who owed his career to none of the advantages of family, favour or fortune.

So, my friends, the *outsider* who succeeded on merit alone.

Sensitive and immensely likeable. Funny and rhetorical.

The Master of Sweet Reason and the ablest speaker of his time.

No one in the last hundred years was more skilled in persuading a jury.

And if you want to bring *change* – to peoples, policies, ideas, remember that a fine advocate still can make a difference.

At the Bar, which he loved, he was simply Norman Birkett Kings Counsel.
A name to respect – and to cherish
A name to praise.
A name to remember.

Goodnight.

Close book – exit

Final Cue - Music